The Bindery

The Bindery

SHANE RHODES

NeWest Press

NeWest Press
201–8540–109 Street
Edmonton, Alberta T6G 1E6
(780) 432-9427
www.newestpress.com

NeWest Press acknowledges
the support of the Canada
Council for the Arts and the
Alberta Foundation for the
Arts, and the Edmonton Arts
Council for our publishing
program. We also acknowledge
the financial support of the
Government of Canada through
the Book Publishing Industry
Development Program (BPIDP)
for our publishing activities.

LIBRARY AND ARCHIVES OF
CANADA CATALOGUING IN
PUBLICATION:

Rhodes, Shane, 1973–
  The bindery / Shane Rhodes.
ISBN-13: 978-1-897126-14-1
ISBN-10: 1-897126-14-X

  I   Title.

PS8585.H568B46 2007
C811'.6   C2006-905265-4

Board Editor: Douglas Barbour.
Cover and interior design:
  Jason Dewinetz.
Cover image: iStockPhoto.

NeWest Press is committed to
protecting the environment
and to the responsible use of
natural resources. This book is
printed on 100% post-consumer
recycled and ancient-forest-
friendly paper. For more
information, please visit
www.oldgrowthfree.com

Printed and bound in Canada.

1 2 3 4 5 | 10 09 08 07

Canada Council Conseil des Arts
for the Arts   du Canada

Canadian   Patrimoine
Heritage   canadien

edmonton
arts
council

ACKNOWLEDGEMENTS

I would like to thank the following people for their help, sug-
gestions and encouragement: Nancy Batty, Clair Batty, Chris
Jennings, Ross Leckie, Señora Ramona Lopez, Rajinderpal S.
Pal, Aaron Peck, David Seymour, Sue Sinclair, and Jacqueline
Turner. Thanks as well to the Canada Council for the Arts and
the Alberta Foundation for the Arts for financial support dur-
ing the composition of parts of this book.

Thanks to NeWest Press and my editor, Doug Barbour, for their
work and support of this book. As well, thanks to Jason Dewi-
netz for his nimble-fingered book design.

And to Rebecca, companion, traveller, loved.

Earlier versions of these poems were published in *Alberta
Views*, *Arc*, *Canadian Literature*, *filling Station*, *Ottawater*,
Qwerty, *The Fiddlehead*, *The Malahat Review*, *The Walrus*,
West Coast Line, and a broadside published by above/ground
press. I would like to thank the editors.

A limited edition chapbook entitled *Tengo Sed* — based upon
the second section of this book — and designed by Jason
Dewinetz of Greenboathouse Books — won second place in the
limited edition category at the Alcuin Society's 23rd Annual
Awards for Excellence in Book Design in Canada.

"*Ocurrió en el tiempo de las noches largas y los vientos de hielo: una mañana floreció el jazmin del Cabo, en el jardin de mi casa, y el aire frío se impregnó de su aroma, y ese día también floreció el ciruelo y despertaron las tortugas.*

Fue un error, y poco duró. Pero gracias al error, el jazmin, el ciruelo y las tortugas pudieron creer que alguna vez se acabará el invierno. Y yo también."

LAS PALABRAS ANDANTES
Eduardo Galeano

1

If it was the sea we heard, it was the sea
and not the sea, water lapped the edge of rock,
filling our nights with tidings of the sea
which was not the sea but a lack of sound, a lake.
If it was a man who ran on the sand beside the sea
which was not the sea but a gulf of water round
where a man was running hard, it was his water,
and then it wasn't and then it was again.

If it was the sea we heard, it was our hearing
built its hooded anemones, its ancient mouth
saying nothing we could hope to see,
it was the sea with a tongue upon the trees
which lingered round the lake
and moved to a shrinking thought.

If it was the sea we heard
when we heard the sea, it was a sound
beyond the contrivance of an ear,
a conch raised to the air's constant
clot and quaver we could raise and carry
to dry inland houses as if a plenum crust
of jellied water. And we would think
how that day, the sea, a driftwood log,
footprints filled with water.

If a woman walked beside the water,
the names we gave to shells
were as strange as the names we gave to her.
She sank in the sand of the plenitude of the sea
and we sang for such was the way
when by the diminished sea.

If we knew, it was the sea we knew
and not what the sea was singing
(the sea does not sing, the sea is not me)
if it was the sea we followed
note for note, each wave breaking
the back of the other.

IF IT WAS THE SEA WE HEARD
Penelope's Song

Whose sea?

The sun up this early and how.

Going forth from the knees to a truant happiness.

Will be finished in one tall order, they assured us, pecking wives on cheeks, rubbing the curly heads of children.

The rustle of wind through sheep shit and sand flies. The usural torpidity of the morning and its general direction of decay.

A moment's density in their eyes offered up the shy event of our reckoning to a pampered heart.

They took long oars to water as the end of privileges of place and turned heels to breaker with morning sun upon the rosined water, their bodies hip-deep in the swelling surf.

Through the surf's ebb and draw, they moved the stalwart ship.

Every utterance we gave was the true one.

They set sail to wind, canvas snapping.

As they moved into the furthest wave with its broken back upon the buried reef, blue water from sudden depths beyond the shifts and shoals of doubt, our hands tired.

We turned our backs upon the ocean roar.

These men over the ocean's small but growing depths, I remember.

Of doubt, these soiled ghosts?

Theirs was the calm of raging waters, fettered by borders of acceptable blame.

The end I see in this old order dismantled nightly, step for step ahead, to an end greeded by sleep.

Much doesn't care for my place in this story of unlikely return.

A tearmoist body a man could wreck against.

Night ravels me.

2

"'It's a newspaper printed in Spanish,' I said to myself again. 'It's only natural that I don't understand the sound it's making.' Then I really felt I was in exile, and my nervousness was going to make me permeable to what—for want of other words — I shall call poetry."

A THIEF'S JOURNAL
Jean Genet

I write *marigolds in a clear vase* and hope by these words to contain it. By *it* I mean she had left three nights ago and now I miss her. She carries through my thought like the Spanish opera coming through my window: strangeness, missing and knowing song is no relief only the transition of a private worry to an unconjugated public domain.

The sea and its unending labour, the wind and its constant generalization of heat.

As if, in a revolution almost complete but before the final blow where the last city falls, the army of Mayan peasants were to put down their guns and return home to plant corn — for it is spring and unplanted seed shames the dirt. In a year, the peasants would be slaves again to the *mestizo* landowners and the dream of a homeland would fade to myth. As if I were to inhabit the suspended animation of that *as if.*

A fidelity beyond the reason I hear — the white pearl of moon, for instance, the coarseness of pubic hair to the touch.

The fish market counters piled high with calico orange snapper, sky-grey grouper and sea bass. They lie on the counters, mouths agasp, glossy eyes turning creamy white as, one by one, the fishmonger scales them and fillets them alive.

Which surprised me the way the trays of fried shark meat surprised me when I saw them in the market beneath the picture of a seven-foot reefshark eating a human leg.

Like a 17th century still-life of fruit so ripe eating it would be a step down from an imagined taste or old morality plays in which one plays the beggar and another the glutton.

I have seen the dried blossoms of marigold strewn in geometric patterns around the graves. Dried, they cauterize wounds and guide the spirit home. Or, as Gerard says, they "cureth the trembling of the heart."

Their name in Spanish is *caléndula* from the Latin *calend* for the end of the month when they were thought to flower (like a woman) most strongly. But they make more sense to me in English as marigold, marsh gold, Mary's gold, the gold of the Virgin.

But switching languages does not get closer to what I mean, for, if anything, the change shows I do not know what I mean. I say *espero* from the Spanish verb *esperar* which means *to hope* or *to wish*

but which also means *to wait*.

The week before, her husband carried on his back from the
market two 30 pound sacks of camotes or purple yams. On
the day before the Day of the Dead, she cleans the camotes
and, on a large charcoal fire in her outdoor kitchen, boils them
until cooked. When cool, she peels and grinds them, or her
daughters do, on the metate, a long grinding board and rolling
pin hewn of volcanic rock. When the camote pulp is fine and
paste-like, she puts it in a large copper kettle with water, sugar
and colouring and boils it to a thick, pink paste. This work
lasts all day and well into the night. Her face and the faces of
her daughters can be seen in the black stone kitchen fanning
the fire which billows smoke. Their arms and faces dotted with
pink miel de camote as it spits over the flame. No light except
the light on their faces from the burning coals. It is hard work
and, by the time they are done and all the pots and even some
tea cups and mugs are filled with the camote, they are tired.
But it must be made or the dead will go malnourished for the
Day of the Dead is their only day back in this world. The fam-
ily sets out food and treats (tobacco, tequila, salt) and dried
flowers. The food is sugary but bland. Sugary for their spirits
are like children and will only be attracted to the sweet. Bland
for, somehow, the dead have already taken the flavour from
it. And to commiserate with the dead, the family must also eat
the sweet, bland food, which they do for the entire week after.
Morning, noon and night they pile the special sweet white
bread with mounds of camote and eat. They eat camote until
they are full. They eat camote until they are tired. They try to
give it away but instead are given more. They try to forget about
it and when they forget about it, it is still on their plates. Every
morning their bread piled high with camote and they eat. They
eat until they are ready to die of it.

TENGO SED

a Señora Ramona Lopez

To have aguamiel, it needs to be stored in a terra cotta cistern (*hecho de barro*) which will keep it cool (*frío*), and that cistern needs (*debe*) to be stopped with a rolled maguey leaf so it can breath (*respirar*) but not spill, and it all needs to be brought to town (*al pueblo*) on the back of a mule (*un burro*). But this stuff in plastic (*plástico*) jugs tied to a bicycle, she says (*me dice*), I wouldn't wash my dog (*lavar mi perro*) with it. When she was a child (*una niña*), every morning (*cada mañana*), she says, they would drink aguamiel (*tomábamos aguamiel*), a sweet greyish-green sap from the maguey cactus. It kept them healthy (*para nuestra salud*). With every meal her family would eat nopal (*nopales*), a thinner, leaf-like cactus cultivated on the sierra with chilli (*con chili*), tomato (*jitomate*), onion (*cebolla*), garlic (*ajo*) and a pinch of salt (*sal*). It kept us healthy. When the men wanted to get drunk (*emborracharse*), they drank (*tomaron*) pulque which was fermented aguamiel. When they wanted to get really drunk (*casi muertos*), they drank mescal which was something like (*un poco como*) pulque but distilled (*más fuerte*). But now she says, you cannot even buy the stuff (*no se puede comprarlo*). A boy (*hay un chico viene*) comes every morning (*cada mañana*) from the campo (*del campo*) with two four-litre plastic jugs of pulque and aguamiel tied to his bicycle. But this is not right (*pero, no está bien*), she says (*me dice*).

I would buy the light that falls through the stained glass windows of these old churches.

> Flying into Mexico City from Merída, a long brown thread of smoke hangs over the crater of Popocatépetel.

I would join this economic union, here, at your hip.

> We took the same path as Cortez but 30,000 feet higher — in from the Gulf at what he named the Villa Rica de la Vera Cruz, then west through the mountain passes and plains. A passage replete with historical rhyme: foreign tankers full of Pemex crude and the stink of Conquistadors under full heat in full armour — soldiers whose only promise was looted gold while the ships to take it home were scuttled in the harbour.

I would market the shouts of these women who live in the street.

> The plane banks to the left and the passengers slump into their accumulated momentum. When the Spanish came to the volcano Popocatépetel in 1521, the Conquistador _____ was lowered into the crater with a bucket and a hammer, indigenous guides above guiding the rope through the hot rocks. He came back to the surface with a pail full of sulphur — (he would die ____ years later, in _____, destitute and _____)(this is history speaking) — to make gunpowder for the arquebus and cannon.

I would privatize this rain water puddle.

> Which gave them Tenochtitlan the first time.

I would sell this music coming through the cantina windows.

So many Conquistadores drowned in Largo Texcoco on
the Noche Triste — unable to swim, their clothes so laden
with gold.

I would steal this history.

More buckets were lowered into the volcano, and the
volcano ate them.

We hiked all morning to get there. Up through
pine trees and jumbled scree, thick mattresses
of moss sucking at the summer storms.
At the top of the mountain ridge and to the north
a spooned-out hollow full to our feet
of blowing cloud, while, to the south, the sky
was clear and blank. And it seemed — walking
across that ridge — our feet slipping on shale
and mid-summer snow green with rock-dust —
we moved as light moves, on the constant
brink between two wholes incommensurate.
If you want something five times more distant,
said Leonardo, *paint it five times more blue.*

We descended in late afternoon, down through
the shrill screech of pika, high mountain meadows
with their last crescents of snow.
The hard religious hunger of rock-bound roots.
A feeling, then, of life bedded down deep
within itself. We had argued all day
and only now did a peace ascend to meet us
as the snowmelt flowed in an ermine-like lather
down through the valley below
where children filled with the rapture
of Guadalupe-Tonantzin appearing high
in the enamelled pine.
And when we returned to the city,
there were the signs and sounds cities make:
clink of cutlery, men on street corners
laughing and exchanging money.
Children played with summer-intensity
last games of tag. Everything still happened
for the first time.

They agreed, hiking the mountain which over-looked the city spires and silver mines, that their lives were already arthritic with worry.

On the mountaintop, they removed t-shirts, jeans and under-wear to suntan — interrupted only by the goat herds eating brown grass dried tough by summer drought.

And they meant by "worry" an anxiety fed from its own imprecision and so became an italicised *sadness* — as in a life corroded by work, the lack of money, the loss of time.

With an afternoon rain shower, they dried themselves and descended, stopping only to pick cactus fruit — its cool skin and warm, lucent centre full of pits.

"This is how the middle-aged would live," he would say at times. "A life of pattern and routine with very little conscious waste."

And it makes me want a quick end to it: "They returned to their pension (the one with the beaten tile in every room), made dinner and turned out the lights" or "The grey/green pigeons, startled by the evening bells, flew from the gutters to the church spires."

Instead: in a restaurant that night, they ate green poblano chillies fried in batter and stuffed with meat, raisins and walnuts and topped with walnut nougat and pomegranate seeds.

A nun created the dish in 1826 to honour the ten-month despot rule of Augustin de Iturbide, self-claimed ruler of New Spain — deposed, exiled, returned, arrested, hung.

After, they drank coffee picked from mountains in Michoacán and brought up through Uruapan.

In its form, the restaurant mimicked Iglesia de San Cayetano — built by a Spanish silver baron as thanks to the commercial graces of a saint rather than the indigenous slaves who worked the mines below.

But that is not all: the señora in Progreso said, looking from the government dock built for the luxury cruise ships to the surrounding mansions of the local rich, "Salinas was a crook! But he was lucky crook — the *cabrón* now lives in Ireland!"

In the painting of Saint Francis in El Convento de Guadalupe just outside of Zacatecas, the anonymous landscape is of an imagined Europe — far off hills with tended sheep, oak forest, a small stream, a dream of homeland. The colours of the painting are dark greens and tar-oil blacks aged by the light and dry air as if to prove a heaven should be composed only of light. The convent was built by the Franciscans in the 19th century and called El Colegio Apostólica de Propaganda Fide — the padres in their brown cowled shawls in the wind-kept deserts to the north. By the 19th century, it would have been unclear for whom they were apostlating. The light through the windows now is full of a blue that will fill the streets with sleeping dogs. Bells continue to ring from the high campanile for morning mass, linked by a long rope of sisal to a padre in the plaza below. He pulls on the rope, gathering what remains of the faithful.

The main cobbled street filled with horses, men and women
in costume. On one side, the Conservatives. On the other, the
Liberals. Or, the Spanish and the Mexicans. Or, those for the
crown and those against it. On the Mexican uniforms, women
have pinned small garlands of fruit and membrillos, a wild
apple that grows in the surrounding hills. The air tinned with
the smell of gunpowder. With a trumpet call, the Conserva-
tives charge and the Liberals retreat. Dust and the exaggerated
features of men playing fear. Then the action stops and the
Liberals charge back. The sound of rushing horses and the
exaggerated features of men playing victory. When the battle
is finally over, a marching band of second-hand suits, trumpets
and an old beaten tuba begins to play. A straw-stuffed general
hangs from one corner of the stage. The vanquished dance with
the victors. Men dance with men. Women dance with women.
Someone dances with a dog. False moustaches and beards are
ripped off as bottles of mescal pass from mouth to mouth, the
rims shined with spit. Gunshots become less coordinated and
more frequent. At the only cantina in town, a man, still on his
horse, rides halfway through the door and asks for a bottle of
beer. At the corner urinal and grinning at the horse, a man lets
go a torrent of piss.

In the evenings, I ran. The glabrous
skin of cactus in headlights. Dead dogs
wild with larva by the side of the road.
When it rained, water gathered
in small streams that turned to torrents
through the unnavigable streets. In the afternoons,
I avoided the heat and studied Mexican history.
You could walk half an hour from my
pension to the town granary where hung
the severed heads of the rebel leaders
a century before. When the Loyalists
retook the city, they held a 'lottery
of death' for they believed the townsfolk
too compliant. Each winner was tortured
and hung. *The violence of the body*,
says de Certeau, *reaches the page only*
through absence, through what is erased.
And maybe you'd say the same for pleasure.
They met his mother in Sweden where she'd moved
after escaping from Sudan. When she met
his white girlfriend, who he'd been
so proud to present, his mother said to him
later, privately, *Think of her as the kind of woman*
you meet on a train and with whom
you have a wonderful conversation
and, at the next stop, she gets off.
At night, we would hold each other tightly
and when we came our bodies shook
as the light in empty churches shakes
between the volcanic stone. It was chiselled
in the 16th century by indigenous labourers
each with a small raised brand on his cheek.

Two young men play guitar. They play in a small house where bare light bulbs hang from the concrete ceiling. Outside it rains and between breaks in the rain you can hear waves roaring to shore. We are on the Gulf of Mexico and with each wave you can smell the rancid breath of the sea, a mouth that has tasted and eaten everything. One of the guitar players has a cell phone clipped to his belt and behind him, on the wall, is a small shrine to the Virgin of Guadalupe, her brown eyes lowered with all the beatific adoration of an overdose. The men sing traditional songs — *pura yucateca* — to an old man who sits on a blue stool before them. It is his birthday and one of the boys playing guitar is his son who sings with a clear, low voice and wears eyeglasses to look like John Lennon. The old man has eyes that move with the semblance of sight. He has been blind for 27 years and has never seen the son who plays before him. The walls of the house are worn at the level of his hands. He sits before the singers and around him are the people who have gathered to celebrate his birthday. Somebody begins to dance and they sing louder. There is food. There is beer. He is dying. They sing old songs not to please the old man but because everybody sings old songs. He mouths the words he knows and teaches the singers new songs they don't know. He is another year older. He is crying.

CARNE

In a market in Mexico City, vendors sell tacos made from the meat of cooked goat heads. Beside the grills are piles of eyeless sockets and obstinate looking jaws still with their full array of stained teeth. You eat the meat from the head, a man tells me pointing at a skull while pushing a taco deep into his mouth, because then at least you know it's not rat meat.

Señor Lopez had a problem. His back hurt. Not just pain but a pain that would not go away. Nothing would tempt it out of his muscles and bones where it lay like a trodden upon snake. It hurt him when he worked. It hurt him when he screwed. It hurt him when he rested. His wife told him to go to the woman who lived on the edge of the campo. He went to her and said, I think somebody has put a curse on me. She said, let me see, and dealt him his cards. Somebody has put a curse on you, she said. To rid yourself of the curse, make a tea from these herbs and drink it for a week. At the end of the week, kill a chicken and sprinkle its blood on the ground outside your door, then throw the chicken away. Señor Lopez thanked her many times — always leave on good terms with your bruja, your witch — and went away. Señor Lopez drank the tea. Señor Lopez killed the chicken and — when no one was looking—sprinkled its blood outside his door. When he was done, he threw the chicken away. Señor Lopez' back is fine again.

The wind blew at just under 300 kilometres per hour. Even on the shallow shore, the waves and tide swell had reached 13 feet. When the family returned to their house after waiting out the hurricane further inland, there was nothing left. The waves had entered and left each room and taken everything with it. Doors, television, gas stove, fridge, curtains, carpets, stamps, forks, spoons, pictures. The only thing left behind was beach sand which had piled up the walls to the rafters. Even fifteen years after the hurricane, everyone still keeps their important pictures and letters in small sacks hung at the end of their beds so they can be grabbed quickly. The family buys nothing that can't be easily left behind. They work as landlords in the town, renting summer houses to winter foreigners like me. But, she says, this Yucateca woman in her sixties who still remembers living with her mother in a small Mayan cabaña with dirt floors, the sea is our landlord, our dueña.

Women dance around men
    who are also dancing in a way —
        this corner
that corner
        sidestep
    justice
the anointed bones.
    The bartender
        at the back of the bar
is cool
    and barely awake.
        He pours tequila
into shot glasses
    the amber colour
        of palm oil.
Already the day is full:
    the despot general
        paraded his amputated leg
through the streets
    while the American bureaucrats
        — appalled —
applaud
    oaths
        sanitary adjectives
trainloads of armaments
    and the rustle
of assassins in the woods.
    Light shimmers
        from disco balls
that remember nothing
    to the man in the corner
        grinding
against his partner's torso.
    He must be Economic Liberalization
        and she the Working Poor.

No, he's the World Bank
    and she Monetary Transcendence
and Devaluation.
    But you are a tourist here —
        you look
and look away.

For anyone who has been sung to in Hebrew by a naked Israeli
    at 2 in the morning.

For the girl learning Spanish from English who only spoke
    Japanese.

For there are boys in Orissa playing cricket with the sea.

For the seventy caged birds at the small pension in which we
    stayed that, every morning, woke us with song.

For the Amritisar-Howrah-Amritsar Mail and our 20 hours
    thereon, thereon, thereon.

For the man on a street corner selling his amazing invention
    that kills rats *and* cockroaches for only 6 pesos.

For only 6 pesos.

For, in Mexican Spanish, *"me late"* means *I like it,* or, literally, *it
makes my heart beat.*

For only that which goes on hurting will be remembered.

For the man who said I looked like George Michael and then
    sang "Careless Whisper" stopping, at appropriate pauses, for
    my approval.

For yak cheese hung out to dry in the wind.

For the only way to kill a cockroach, I have found, is to tell it
    stories of depravity.

For, when you have everything and nothing, it's only the noth-
    ing that hurts.

For the Mexican bus driver who stopped in the middle of a
    busy street and, with an array of honks and complicated
    hand gestures, made a date with the woman working cash at
    a convenience store.

For those who make love in overnight buses thinking the other
    passengers do not hear.

For the temple baboons threatening the faithful with their
    angry red asses.

For it is so still in this room / even the razors sleep.

For the sound of a spider chasing a cricket across a marble floor.

For, here, *Castles* become *Elephants* and *Queens* merely *Advi-
sors.*

For there are prayer flags even the wind can't read.

For I am as still, tonight, as Pascal sitting in an empty room.

For the old women in the market selling fried grasshoppers
from the pockets of their aprons.

For high up in the Himalayas / you open the door / the clouds
come in.

For the village family who named their son *Usmail* after an
envelope carrying the stamps of a foreign country.

es como un plano / de mis humiliaciones y fracasos"— I read
from a copy of Borges I bought in a tienda for 20 pesos.

My hostel room on Hipólito Yrigoyen just down from Plaza de
Mayo is cheap because it's beside a porn cinema. All day and
night, street noises mix with the long lingering polyglot moans
of faked female orgasm.

In 1946, Perón appointed Borges the "Inspector of Poultry and
Rabbits in the Public Markets," as an insult.

Three decades later, Borges was appointed director of the Bib-
lioteca Nacional, which was built on the razed deathbed home
of Eva Perón as an insult.

As the sex throb thuds through the hostel wall, I think of how
this city is like a library to me, its streets a plan of humiliations
and failure.

In the square before the presidential palace, grandmothers tie
white bandanas on the trees or carry pictures of their children
to remember how the government tortured them and threw
the bodies to the sea.

"In endeavouring to describe these scenes of violence, one is
tempted to pass from one simile to another," wrote Darwin in
his journal in 1834 while hiking through the Pampas.

As he grew older and blind, Borges wrote more poetry (for he
could carry poems in his head) and paid young men to read to
him.

Two men in a room — one reading stories he does not know;
the other listening to the stories he knows but cannot see.

Is this history?

When he was old, a writer from Argentina says on the radio, recounting the literati before and after the coup, *Borges became a fool, believing what other people told him, shaking hands with Pinochet.*

Here is a coast. Here is a harbour.
Here is beach sand. Here is owned land.
Here is an economist. Here is a fine mist.
Here is a dock. Here is a flock of birds.
Here is a trade. Here is a woman in labour.
Here is trade. Here is a woman's labour.
Here is a border zone. Here is a pay phone.
Here is free trade. Here is a man getting paid.
Here is a market place. Here is its church.
Here is its steeple. Here is nada para amor.
Here is a calle. Here is a detalle.
Here is a mercado. Here is a SuperMercado.
Here is a Zapatista. Here is a Pípila.
Here is a revolucionario. Here is a federalista.
Here is a trabajador. Here is your zapato.
Here is 200 murdered women.
Here is a fábrica. Here is some maquillaje.
Here is a turista. Here is an assembly line.
Here is an assembled line. Here is the blazing divine.
Here is a smokestack. Here is a wire rack.
Here is product X purchased at £100.
Here is a statue to commemorate. Here is a statute to commiserate.
Here is the policía. Here is the beautiful song.
Here is the beautiful song. Here is the beautiful song.
Here is a room. Here is a man sitting.
Here is his hammock. Here is his beach sand.
Here is his coast. Here is his harbour.

3

A PICTURE BY BRUEGHEL:
LANDSCAPE WITH ICARUS FALLING
contra Auden

Brueghel was right—
everyone sees
nothing at least
once in the life
of a tragedy.
To the left,
in the painting,
the tenant farmer
walks behind a horse—
four centuries
of ploughing
and not once
has he dropped
his seed.
The light here
will be taken
without footnote
by Monet.
Yet the fallen
boy beating
the sea with
broken wings
is less
amazing
than the ship
sailing by
with its paint-thick hold
full of slaves
from Mozambique.
The shepherd
stares away so
intent on nothing
his eyes
gouge out.
Such private things
done
with public weight.

He was wrong,
the old master,
about suffering.
It does not ascend
beyond this human
position —
like Icarus to myth —
but profits
beneath paint
(a scream through water)
in parenthesis.

THE FOUR CAPTIVES
OF THE BOBOLI GARDENS
(four statues by Michelangelo)

In this life, much goes unfinished.
    Rock falls
            from one form to another,
filling the workshop floor
        and the statues are
            bent as, even in sleep,
they carry the burden
        upon them.
                Oblivious to evening light
caught in their curves, art breaks
        its bones
            on the slow slavery
of matter.
        Yet they taught us well
            these statue-instructors,
their completions
        so complex one only thinks
            of thinking of it.
            We could coax them
out, teach them
        the lines of this world:
hold the tool like so,
        the pope's sepulchre
            is planned from conclave,
we call those moons
        the Medician stars,
            and grow weary
of perfection and drown
            in our mirrors. Or leave them
informis, "in the rough,"
            as Vasari said,
beneath a corpus of stone.
        Like a figure
            in Pompeii.

Like a body's mineral numbness.
        Or lose
                yourself
in the captured details:
        lump of rock
                nothing like the beard
it is, or imagine the sculptor
        at night, candle
                on a paper hat
forehead gathering wax
        and rock dust
                as the marble broke
before him.
        When he died, his body refused
                to rot
or so said those
        who pushed aside the granite top.
                There are restrictions, too,
in how far we can push
        this form.
For we are here,
        not the gardens of Boboli
                or even the Museo Nazionale
where guards sleep
        by the masterpiece,
                night falls
like a hammer
        and the marble is,
                in the way of marble,
senseless.

so I've packaged together
a unique set of tools
any land-based eating establishment
a work of art
a great frame
best to worst
I started by ranking
this non-surgical procedure
done in the doctor's office
a few hours later
you'll see the results
a great art
a work of frame
placed by a gush
centrist docility
decision should be based on comfort
and which of these 17 countries
should I suggest
when selecting your fabric
you have to give him credit
he's tough on terrorism
on record
wrinkle resistant
god knows they've used it
to study the problem further
I'd just like to say
glory seeking officials are probing
he exhorts
these guys have stayed too long
as usual
I can afford the price tag
more than anything
it was the hat
you'd like a hat like that
determine your price range
find a reputable banker
then someone you can trust

spend more and they'll rave
for her global mail-order service
this confusing episode demonstrates
the self-esteem of an oppressed group
I'm not going to argue
free markets are intrinsically
free
turn this up and you'll feel
world domination seems certain
like you're behind
and liking it
finally think romance
after all these pants
the curve of his face
I'd just like to say
the past 34 years
have been the best
but chief one arrow proved them wrong
you could actually quote him
saying fuck
parts of the treaty were edited here
a ceremony made up in warmth
what it lacked in honesty
he smiled
wept a little
screwed the lease
you the investor
sitting over there
sure you know about love
but you never know about Italy
the tale begins in Brooklyn
he's on the surgeon's table
all he saw was crumbs
anesthesiologists with name tags
passing gas
and studying the monitors
half the fun was getting there

even better the weather channel
a raincoat an umbrella
snails supposedly accompanied by focaccia
the great masticator
minimized bowel movements
in his office chair
I do think there are economic forces
at work here
we get down
we grease the machine
to subtly illustrate
there are some studies
in whose fictions
we are achieved
so let's discuss how our money works
dick's filling in for lisa
he remembers his visa
fed the skinny end in
if he'd been a little more clever
he'd own a little country
on the salary of a rookie
out of dumb luck — fat chance
I'm a government man
I blow dry
I spend a lot less time
brushing the wrong way

Around doubt,
respect.

Around love,
roses,

debt.
Much industrial

share-sweat
has brought them

to you. Frothed
Persian light.

The salesman's
semen-sweet fête.

Let down, then,
your beautiful

tabernacle
said I (& Blake).

God?
Profit

margin?
This hint

of mould
your undoing.

Love?
Spare me.

There's
so little

time
left.

Sleep, a kind of Scarborough,
a mulch of the aberrant,

the attainable
which our bodies brim.

Poor life — given
but not taken, taken

but never taken away.
A psalmody to mellow the wind.

What, then, of mysticism?

What of the spirit buzzing
in the high transformers?

What of the bittersweet?
Our seeing has weight.

And as the bomb falls

on the white sands
of Alamogordo,

it falls the way a mind
in mid-age falls

firmly around the dream
it has of itself.

Uranium collapses
on a deuterium core.

I touch the fine groove
of a name or a date or a reason.

4

"To think is to perform an act. In order to act, you have to discard frivolity and set your idea on a solid base. So she was aided by the idea of solidity, which she associated with the idea of virility, and it was in grammar that she found it near at hand."

OUR LADY OF THE FLOWERS
Jean Genet

1. Leaves elm of shadow by the mottled porch her grand-
   mother and my letters a white hand writing this goes over
   the wind

2. There were no fish because (so we were told by a man in a
   restaurant later that day as — raising his coffee mug to his
   mouth — he said, in a practised whisper, as between the
   tourist and the unemployed) there are no fish.

3. And who could write a love poem better than Issa? I weep
   because it has been said!

   > *Were it but sweet it would be*
   > > *my dew*
   > *his dew.*

4. *Man is more than likely descended from the apes than
   from the angels* or so thought Darwin on a boat in the
   middle of the Pacific after watching the agonizing slow
   copulation of tortoises in the year 1835 of our Lord.

5. Like uranium and its slow journey into lead.

6. Poetry

   a. William Carlos Williams: Poetry should be written
      in "the speech of Polish mothers." Which makes sense
      from a paediatrician living near Paterson, New Jersey
      with 1/3 of its population foreign-born whites.

   b. Pound: "Make It New" in the soap scum on the side of
      a bathtub.

7.   Cuddle me
blond boys
    in hoodies

          your kisses
     sugar & sophistry
        wear our shame

as Troy in spirit.

8. How early Flemish religious paintings showed oranges instead of apples because apple, as a word, had not yet been translated.

9. Separate, as St. Augustine says, that which knows from that which knows itself.

    a. Or separate, as the distance, say, between what you want and what you are willing to do to get it.

    b. Or between the woodpecker and the dead spruce stump it taps in the clearcut.

10. The day before we had marched in a demonstration against Talisman and Shell Oil.

11. Cherry blossoms
through the chain
link fence.

12. We laid a blanket on the grass on Nose Hill and watched the northern lights, smoked pot and shivered. It was fall, the lights at their most intense, full of flourescent greens and blues like metal filings flung into deep water. On the blanket, we held each other to keep warm.

13. But I am awake in this world, not sleeping, not dreaming . . .

14. Napoleon writing to Josephine and telling her not to wash as he returned over the long barren paths from the Russian front. He wanted the smell of her cunt, the salt of her on his tongue. And I am thinking right now of how exactly I would write that in a letter.

15. Gertrude Stein: "Remarks are not literature."

16. If money moves so freely, why not people? (¿Y si el dinero se mueve tan libremente, porque no la gente?)

17. When French explorers reached the rapids of the upper St. Lawrence and could go no further, they named the rapids (as they are still called today) and all land to the west: *Lachine — La Chine — China.*

18. The window is . . . The table is . . .
    The doorway through which she entered is . . .

19. Each freedom and its geometry of restraint, each beauty with its allotted gravity. Katherine in law school saying, over a beer, she can't stand this shit, another theory to take the world apart with nothing left to put it back together.

20. All day, the wind spoke to the sea
    in cursive script and the wind took its letters
    to the shore and the sand which
    remembered the sea and the wind
    and then it forgot and then it remembered
    and then it forgot again.

21. As Wittgenstein says — almost as an afterthought —"What is thinkable is possible too."

22. Small song, words laid out in the dark that each voice must take up before the meal is our own.

23. The silver fish you saw in the bay   Reflection of a smoke-
stack in a mountain lake   This uranium-rich country, here,
at your arm

24. Do you still believe
we can undo
all that has been done
and do right
with all we have done wrong—
Andrew on the pier
throws seashells
back into the sea.

25. a. . . . following the easterly range of the mountains, to
the source of the main branch of the Red Deer River;
thence down the said river, with the stream, to the
junction therewith of the outlet of the river, being
the outlet of the Buffalo Lake; thence due east twenty
miles; thence on a straight line south-eastwardly to the
mouth of the said Red Deer River on the south branch
of the Saskatchewan River; thence eastwardly and
northwardly, following on the boundaries of the tracts
conceded by the several treaties numbered four and
five to the place of beginning. . . .

b. MERIDIAN 4; RANGE 24; TOWNSHIP 40; SEC-
TION 21; QUARTER SOUTH WEST

26.   This, my Arcadia,
                                    lashed
        to the lamp post!

27. In medieval times, the betrothed would sleep side by side
for three days before the wedding—naked and with only a
sharpened sword laid on the mattress between them.

28. There is something of freedom that freedom lacks.

29. Advice from a Texan in Mexico: "My grandpa said there were three things to know in life: how to drink, how to dance, some names to call the stars."

30. Morning's menarche

31. A girl dressed in white playing hopscotch among the labourers in a field. Her squares outlined with yellow corn seed. The brown backs of men and women bent in work around her.

32. My aunt's escape from East Germany at the end of the war: her family lived for two weeks on stolen potatoes and eggs as they walked by night beneath the searchlights and razor wire to a new line floating above the dirt.

    a. That country no longer exists, yet my aunt is still living.

    b. A story, like most, built by absences and fleeing.

33. "And whoever thinks that by including this story my sole aim was not merely filling space on paper and reducing slightly the enormous number of white pages before me, is sorely mistaken," said Gombrowicz.

34. The yellow bird I saw this morning before light climbed into the valley, suspended, barely moving from cactus to cactus, sucking nectar between the thorns.

35. Be public, be private, be anything but alone.

36. a. . . . 2 large wooden bins each of maize, beans, sage and
      purslane seeds; 1,200 loads of wood . . .

    b. *Los Pescadores y Los Rancheros*

       The rancher ranches so every two months
       he can drive to town and eat shrimp
       with beer and batter and cocktail sauce.

                 The fisherman fishes
                 for an occasional meal
                 of chicken and veal.

37. When a woman comes, who can stand the wooing?

38. I want to remember, now, the small wounds of your body,
    the places where you let my body in — a space without
    geometry where Pythagoras would weep, Euclid take out
    his eyes with a compass point.

39. "The body having been carried with so beautiful a train
    into S. Croce where the above-named Lieutenant, who
    had been present in virtue of his office, thinking to do a
    thing pleasing to many, and also (as he afterwards con-
    fessed) desiring to see in death one whom he had not seen
    in life then resolved to have the coffin opened. This done,
    when he and all the rest of us present thought to find the
    body already marred and putrefied, because Michelangelo
    had been dead twenty-five days and twenty-two in the
    coffin, we found it so perfect in every part, and so free
    from any noisome odor, that we were ready to believe that
    it was rather at rest . . .

40. Galileo tries to measure longitude
    at sea with his new machine.
    With one eye focussed on Jupiter,
    the other searches a ground glass
    for its unwinding moons.
    But it's no use, he writes in his journal,
    for even a heart beat
    makes the planet shake
    from the calm harbours of Livorno.

41. Is it enough to see clearly and to be stained by what we
    see?

42. to sell and sell quickly

    a. "Error" graffitied in large block letters on an overpass
       bridge.

43. . . . in a sweet and most peaceful sleep."

44. Because, in the movies, there would be backlighting.

45. No telephone. Just books,
    open windows, and a radio
    to sift the still air. Saskatchewan.
    The CKAU announcer talks
    of "hog futures" and, I think,
    this, indeed, is a kind place.

46. David's story of a Moscow cemetery and how he found
    Pasternak's grave on the anniversary of his death by the
    sound of people reciting poetry.

47. moth wings brush
    the window

    pane   caress
    the dark   compose

    the night

48. And we shovel our voices into the mist soaked air.

49. a. We are midway through the story now: Odysseus
       about to be fucked by Circe.

    b. "I'll be," she said, "your Bikini, your Pacific atoll."

    c.

50. Televisions were new in the town and all the programs
    were in English though everybody spoke Farsi. Those
    with even a small knowledge of English were given the
    task of translation. After several months, though, some
    townspeople realized many of the translators did not
    know English at all but were making new Iranian stories.
    Jack and Krissy in *Three's Company* discussing, intimately,
    the value of the hejab. Fonzie from *Happy Days* worried
    about black market parts for his motorcycle. Gilligan lost,
    somehow, in the Red Sea.

51. Bigger bombs (past the 50 mile radius) did not result in more collateral damage but were wasteful, "needlessly pushing up the atmosphere."

52. Because, in the movies, it would happen fast with slight whistlings of air.

53. you giving
    me head

    this snow
    not so

    barren

54. Because we would be massaging your beautiful feet.

55. Because at Missile Park near the White Sands Missile Range in Santa Fé, New Mexico, security is very, *very* important.

56. Or is it that my uncle laboured all his life so someone could say, in a eulogy, in a funeral home in autumn, "He was a *good worker*?" His body another five pounds of ash for the tired lake.

57. *My* plutonium primer   *Your* plutonium primer

58. Saskatchewan. I live here for a week and count the number of trucks gone by on one hand. Ten species of cacti, two flat tires, twenty-seven deer, one wood stove called New Perfection. Tell me, then, of the things you hate.

59. Somebody has a headache. Somebody rests their head against a cold tail fin.

60. a. Nothing but wheat fields and loneliness

    b. Each particle created in my likeness.

    c. Is this what Blake called *milky fear*?

61. Even now, when she hears sirens, she thinks of hiding.

62. ~~Human thinking *is* error.~~

63.

64.   Even in this cold
                                    you are naked
              so quickly!

65. A grandfather is 70 and his children want to throw him
    a birthday party. He accepts but with the pre-condition
    that the party not be held in his name but in the name of
    a niece or nephew. I have not lived 70 years, he explains,
    by attracting the unneeded attention of gods.

66. Reading this reminds me of the Nisga'a Treaty.

67. a.   The bluebird makes a racket.
                              Is he also hoping
       to get lucky?

    b. "No ideas but in things," wrote William Carlos
       Williams, middle-aged and knee-deep in the polluted
       Passaic.

    c. The Beautiful thing!   vs.   Oh horrid parts!

68.   *On Imitation*

       In the night,
       the cat-in-heat sang.
       In the morning,
       the mockingbird sang
       of the cat-in-heat.
       In the afternoon,
       I wrote of the mockingbird.

69. a. To whom do you tell the things that happen in the
       world?

    b. "You in the dinghy (piccioletta) astern there!"

    c.

70. My grandmother, losing her memory, writes each fact she knows in an alphabetical address book — an order every new morning turns mystical. In her cupboard, she keeps a jar labelled "String, too short to use."

71. This economic union, here, at your hip.

72. Use it not more than once in a hundred said Issa.

73. The drone of a float plane fades to the drone of a mosquito a metre from my head.

74. a. "I am not going to be working with *that* unpleasantry," she says in the Goose Bay-Happy Valley donut shop.

    b. Q Was your pregnancy planned?
       A Not well.

75. The town looks like an outpost, impermanent, on the edge, even, of exile. The buildings, ugly prefabricates, melt into the permafrost. The Inuit and Innu kids wear the shirts and baseball caps of American hockey teams. The poster girl on the sports bar billboard beside the main street is thin, blue-eyed and pink-white.

76. Or, as Ka-Payak-Waskunam said, "

77. Only what you love remains.

    a. Thorarche of morning snow

78. Heraclitus may have said you cannot step into the same river twice — which is a way of saying you can't even do it once (Li Po).

79. These strings of honey, these strings of steel, notes rising from the sound box long after the fingers have strummed, up through the poplar leaves, then gone.

80. *And what if we did not imagine the common affiliations of race, language, nation?*

81.   Spring
                            steam rises
            from the shithouse.

82. Or, as Thoreau says, "Beware of all enterprises that require new clothes."

83.   Work. Sudden shower.
                                From the 18th floor of this office tower
            all those umbrellas bloom!

84. But, oh, how the tin wreath sparkles!

85.   This lateral merger, here, on your chest.

86. As St. Augustine says, *"Soon. Presently. Let me wait but a little longer."*

87.   His cock rising from the silk kimono.

88. George W. Bush, 43rd President of the United States, I have nothing but hard words for you from my room (Apartment 2) on Cambridge Street.

89. How splendid these gifts — like the shadow of a bird passing over your hand.

90. And how will you sleep, now, with everything — molecule, desk, pen, coffee cup — whispering *tell me understand me tell me understand me?*

91.   Don't sleep naked
        beside me, David,

                and then talk all night
                of women!

92. You cannot step into the same river once.

93. Here, at least, the uncertainty is pure.

94. After razing the Mayan temple in Mérida, the Conquistadores used the stone to build the base of the new Cathedral.

95. My heart is more inclined to motion than to rest, to sentiment than to true.

          his
96.   X
          mark

97.   Small pieces of the world
                    snap together
          fall apart.

98.   Where are we now, incense stick?
          Fall — this wind which blows
                    your smoke both in and out?

99. Early morning.
          Women walk to their work in the fields.
                Those trees
            glazed by light.

5

ARGUMENT
Isle aux Coudres, Québec

Early morning and workers
rise to their labour. Nothing more

important to the factory owner,
owners, its chairman of the board

whose penstrokes ring out, saying
"The employed and the unemployed,

upon which half will you fall?";
saying, "The thickness of the air

is not the natural resistance
to machines but work left undone,

finish it"; saying, "How can we
assess its worth unless

we smelter its metal?"

The efficiencies spoiling
in the dark asp of my blood.

Counted amongst its standing reserve,
we whose worthless pastime

is poetry? Our words
are the abacus its grief takes.

In the evening, there will be
the smell of sea, again,

an age of Homer, luxury
and the quiet stir of spermicide

in my jeans
beneath the chestnut trees.

ARGUMENT: AN EXPLICATION
Isle aux Coudres, Québec

The first who landed go unrecorded.
The second buried their thin dead
in the thin top soil —
death made the purchase true
just as the tide pushes deep
in these palatable rocks.
It must have been a dream to them
after Europe and its misery,
the sea and its mystery,
the unending smell of men.

I sit watching tankers pass in the dark,
their constellations of light
far off in the river current
carry life's dark matter
from sweatshops in the far east.
Slowly through the night water
they move like trauma.

In the morning, when we wake,
there will be an age of Homer again
and luxury. It will be the time
of gods, when my fathers rose
to the morning shift and ate in the dark
food they could not see.
Now, there is nothing but me
and that inch of darkness
outside me, where my body drowns.
This life will leave few marks
in the ledger or graves
beneath chestnut trees.

6

PAINTBRUSHES
for the Lepchas

The day was hot and my father drove the gravel logging road
through the high mountain pass with its many pot-holes and
small silver creeks that had overrun their edges. My brother
and I were promised, if we were good, we would stop to pick
Indian Paintbrushes.

> Heated pine.
> Lumber dust sifts
> through the open window.

We were let out into a small flat meadow of marsh grasses,
flowers and stunted spruce covered at the base with thick
clumps of moss. The air was tense as steam rose from the heat-
ing muskeg and each purple bloom strained upward in the light.
Indian Paintbrushes. Looking back on it now, it was beautiful
I'm sure, but I remember feeling disappointed. I had literally
expected "paint brushes" and had hoped to paint with them.

> *Whatever being is born,*
> *know it is sprung*
> *through the union of the field*
> *and the knower of the field*

says the *Bhagavad-Gita*. Krishna is not talking of small moun-
tain meadows. Even if he is, Arjuna doesn't care for he prepares,
regretfully, syllable by syllable, for battle. It is an English trans-
lation bought from a bookstore in Darjeeling in the middle of
summer. Cloud swirls in the valleys below. Directly opposite
the bookstore and 70 miles to the northwest starts Kanchen-
junga, the third highest mountain in the world. On any clear
day, it sits on the edge of your vision massive and snow covered.
In the steep valleys below, women labourers, wicker baskets
strapped to their heads, pick the first green flush of orange
pekoe tea (Super Fine Tippy Golden Flowery Orange Pekoe
Number One).

Over a year since
I have heard from you
my friend.

As for grandfather, he is
dead and T'shangu
full of snow.

Which reminded me, when I read it in your letter, of something
I had read once in a travel book. Since the turn of the century,
with the exception of a few foreigners, mountain climbers no
longer summitted (that great mountaineering verb) Kanchen-
junga but always stopped a few metres short. Because the
mountain-top is sacred and not for the foot of man.

Driving through the Rockies, I listen to Hank Wil-
liams and his heart-felt blues in the spring rain while
the mountains turn white to blue as the snowpack melts.
Heart-felt because it was my father's truck and I felt lone-
some that I hadn't seen him in so long. *Heart-felt* because
there is something in the core wailing appeals to.

He sang "Your Cheatin' Heart" on the recording and I
sang the chorus with him, loud, the way one sings in the
late spring with windows open and mountain sheep by
the side of the road. And when I mouthed the words to
myself that night in the mountain town hostel, the kids
around me looked up from their beers and smiled.

Hank Williams, dead at the age of 29 in the back
seat of a Cadillac after alcohol and drugs took too
great a toll (the liner notes tell me) on his heart.

The snowpack that winter had been meagre and already farmers
complained of a coming drought. They wailed in the newspa-
pers, coffee shops and phone-in radio shows as if weather were
a kind of infidelity, a kind of cheatin' to bemoan in public space.

And this unending expanse (would my father call it a *fee-
lin'* or would he just *sit and sigh*?) gives the music its nerv-
ous rhythm and bass. You can hear it in the passing pickup
trucks and taverns, a courageous syncopation pounding
down roll after roll of fenceline across an open plain.

The blues, they say, has the power to purge the heart.

And though the tape was warped by successive years of sum-
mer heat, and though the songs fell into and out of the standard
twelve bar frame, and though my father's farm was up for sale
(land his *sweet daddy* had cleared — *such a beautiful dream*)
and the future was filled with sorrow and drought, I sang.

And the song was relief, prayer to the unfaithful of the un-
faithful, because finally someone had gotten it right: You
sing because you are 28 and killing yourself. You sing be-
cause you are 60 and selling your farm. You sing because the
only easy endings and beginnings are in songs where there
is call and response even when no one listens or responds

and you sing.

SLAUGHTER

A 7 millimetre Mauser
with a hair trigger, oiled to a sheen
through use and gun bluing. A gift
shot through with a pride beyond talk —
you empty yourself into a child,
my father thought.

We took it out for target practice
on Boxing Day, hitting rings
on a plywood sheet. That fall,
a friend and I bought deer tags
and loaded our own shells —
percussion caps sunk deep.

On the third day of season,
we drove to the nearest bush.
Shots of rum steeled us by ounce
to the rifle's weight
(another friend once injected vodka
before stumbling to the bush).

The hair trigger pushed forward
with a click. Three quick shots
at 150 yards lit a burn
in the rifle's metal
and downed a child-sized doe.
We passed her body across

the fence and hacked her neck —
blood blew across the snow
beating like a song fade out.
Strapped the hind hooves
to the barn rafters,
slit the soft belly skin

between the teats, sex and ribs
and stripped the hide. Wrapped
in butcher paper, we froze the meat
for winter. I wrapped the gun in felt
and locked it back in my father's
gun cabinet, the bolt pulled out.

Everything tonight hums in the intensity of its arrival. Crickets in the grass sawing their legs off. The parabolic flight paths of bats frisking the dark corners. Above us, the last stars let out their fire.

I remember my grandfather's last wish to see Hailey's comet, which he had seen as a child. Yet, the summer of the comet's pass, cancer broke away his background life and he fell out of the comet's orrery.

I remember . . . I remember . . . how clumsy the words sound, as if coming from some distant place where language is old, nebulous and imprecise.

The same year my grandfather died, a teacher held binoculars to my face, his other arm raised over my shoulder pointing to the dead flurry of the comet trapped deep in the double lens.

When my grandfather died, my father answered the phone, paused and held the receiver to his chest as he asked my grandmother if she wanted the wedding band removed from her husband's body.

She was silent, looking out the dining room window into the dark. Stunned, I think, by how such simple words — which had been on a long journey towards her — had finally arrived.

Cancer — it hardly had to do with us. Like the woman I met on a beach in Oregon and the long pointed spear she used to gather crabs from amongst the rocks — she held a crab to my face and it trapped in its shell a pale, beating red as its claws clacked at the stick that had run it through.

In the binocular lens, the image of the comet bounced from lens to mirror to eye. Unmoving. Bicarbonate with speed.

My grandmother at the dining room table crying, silently, into her hands while my father stood, silent, holding the telephone.

His father was dead, his mother was crying and he did not know what to do.

WITHIN THE LIMITS HEREIN DEFINED:
A FOUND POEM
(from Treaty Number 6)

at the mouth
of the river
to the north
of the lake
thence west
to its source
on a line
to the head
in the river
thence down
the said
to a point
on a line
with the river
to the source
of the said
thence north
to the point
of the shore
of the lake
thence west
to the limit
thereof
therefrom
thence due
in the river
up the said
against the
stream in the
mountains thence
south to
the source of
the main of
the said with
the stream of
the outlet of
the rapids of

the river
being thence
east then
west thence
a line straight
to the mouth
of the said
river
on the south
branch
thence east
north
following on
the boundaries
of the tracts
conceded
to the place
of beginning

II.

and also
all their rights

titles
privileges

whatsoever
wherever

situated
and being

within
and embracing

more or less
to have

and to hold
forever

South Saskatchewan River at night, blade silver with moon and willow hung. Eight hundred miles before the prairies release (like a lover holding another within) its muddy water to the Arctic Sea.

The weeping willows must have been brought here by the Dutch and German settlers who took the land from the retreating Nitsitapii and Ayisiniwok.

Blackfoot and Cree, we might say.

I know the tree's Latin name (salix babylonica) because I know of Linnaeus (swedish taxonomist) with his mind sharpened beyond scientific rigor. *Babylonica* he named it for the river forded by captives taken from Zion.

> *Upon the willows we hung our harps as, by the*
> *river, we sat down and wept*

Though the tree came from China.

I camped two weeks in the empty farmland below the river's confluence with the Red Deer, a wintering ground of the Plains Cree. My boyfriend picked me up after two weeks, staying the night in a hunting cabin amongst the rifles, gunpowder, skins and decoys of real men.

Drop a willow branch in mud, and it will sprout roots. Drop it into a pail (my grandmother said) with other plant cuttings and they too will take root.

A Cree woman, her legs crippled by diabetes, her face pitted and scarred, living on the streets in Prince George. She told me, as a child she had once been invited by her father, a Chief, to meet the Governor General in Ottawa to renegotiate a treaty.

Chewed willow bark must have been used (until all who knew its uses were gone) during the plagues of small pox, measles and scarlet fever.

But my father went alone, she said, afraid I might swipe the silverware.

Cold ache of the river current and the quiet grip of roots.

We've been asleep so long.

PORTRAIT

A man embarrassed
          by the small movements
his life required
                    as comfortable with women
          as with a can opener,
                    a butter whisk —
he married my grandmother
          at 20
and bought land
                    to bury himself
          deep
                    in the anaemic fuel
of its labour.
          Ownership
pumped their lives
                    through the long mineral haul
          of his body's blood.
                    Oats.
Barley.
          Wheat.
And husbandry.
                    He was dead by 80
          guiding machines
                    around the empty
potential his life became
          which rose
                    in comic book thought-bubbles
          above him
                    or rose
          as the spirit rises
                    in paintings
by El Greco.

          Land thick
with poplar and willow scrub,
                    the Red Deer River cutting

                    like an archaeologist's spade
                                down through the papery shale —
        every inch a summer novel
                            thick with rain.
                Land cut
                                and cleared
                by my grandfather
        and the glacial tide
                                    of his labour.

        Looking at his hands
                        (which were a portrait
        of this land)
                            you could imagine land
                        creased
                                    and crevassed
        as the callus
                        between forefinger
        and thumb —
                            pressed and furrowed with use
                                beyond a body's bind.
        Hands like this
                        would rather hit you
                                    than talk to you.

        Land taken
                        from the retreating Cree
        to the south and north
                            through treaties number 7 and 6
                        every ownership thereafter
                                    another swindle
        of the dammed-up wealth
                        the land acquired.
        When my father farmed,
                            it was land already worried fine
                        with use

                    tilled
            retilled
                    harrowed
and milled
            to a diaphanous dust.

Looking at this land
                    (which was a portrait
            of this man)
                            you can still smell herds
of buffalo
            the dung-coloured wasted dream of them
rotting
                    in blood-soaked fields.
            The wreckage
floats amongst the trees
            of their land —
tractors
                    moraines of rotting grain
            pemmican pounds
                            my family —
each a ghost
            to its original use
and means.
                    I don't know if it's respect
            or degradation I give it
                            (this
            land)
only how a body married
            to its use
                    will bleed
(this
            man).

My grandmother
in the funeral parlour
            sat while his body burnt
saying,
                He was my one
        my only.
                And the space across

which you stare,
            dear reader,
                    is full.

        Sometimes
                with the heat of wanting
to know.

        Sometimes
with the heat
            of knowing.

7

GAMUT

"My lass is braking.
My brass is aching. Come & diminish me, & map my way."

DREAM SONGS
John Berryman

I.

Have I started every apostrophe
to you with the words of a saint?

You got through it, that vague realm
of disease and now things fall back

into the summer of your affection.
We step out of our roles as sufferers

suffering with cheap suits the occasion —
of course, the wine was actually blood

and all transfusions done with water.
But you pushed through it, so hard

you're back in it, the way that happens
the way it does (your self-substantial

fuel spent).
Something in you can't resist

the irresistible latin
chiffon of attention.

True.
True. A needle will penetrate you

so much better than I and the best
will always be our grotesque, the one

we go to haltingly, disgusted yet
thrilled by our dependence —

love's line
declines

(fairest
to a sterile rhyme).

Don't worry, though, the clouds still hover
over us like pictures of clouds

hovering. The air bluer, here,
and cleaner. Still life composing

the simulation in all its
fidelities.

II.

In all its fidelities, the whips applied
with a certain unspeakable joy — that's right,

put the ink away (that debtor's liquid
prison), there's nothing here

you can actually write. Let's keep
for better truancies — dancing boys

are mortal, after all. But that rent-
free freedom? Lunacy of the upper

decks? Yes, I got it, your missive —
Men are ill-conceived,

mind-vexed,
nettled-thieves,

like apples even —
sweetest flesh

bitter seed — and your shoes,
the blue stilettos. Thanks.

And the barbed wire. Again, you pain me.
Sure, I hollowed your name

with grievances of style
but any friendships new were only to feel

how far from you I fell.
Botched, then? A permanent has-been?

Not quite. There's still a couple turns
in me they haven't seen, a phrase or two

to get me places in places like these.
Listen, let not your woman-emptied

name decay while blood thuds
hotly made in your young heart.

That is my seminary of light
where my love, lacking hurt,

and exploration,
begins.

III.

Begins its snowing, you could,
through Nebraska for days, go and never see

such a variegation of sight, such a
possibility of scene. Through the snow,

the tunnel, the sea, the beach, his window, himself —
a place so curved with mirrors nothing

will get out. The messenger all tied up
in the message he's so pleased to relate

— *Bastards, all of them. Each and every one* —
but which he forgets.

I regret those times I used to lead
such private lives when all I had to do

was write (now, I live in inkless graces).
To have it work for us, even

the domestics must dream in their rusted light.
At the end, our order will form a part

from everything as our bodies build that shiny,
new pastoral sheen. We're travelling back,

even though the past, the revisions
the fouled-up dates, us, have screwed it

mightily: the flowers, the vase, the thing.
You and me, that separation

our words row us between.

IV.

As our men row us away, I'll ask him —
have you had enough of this,

as if just stepped out of an Escher print
for a pack of smokes? No wonder

everything is a bit of a mess, a muss, a bother.
You don't own the copyright to loneliness,

remember? You sold it to me
with that run-down farm, that old Chevy

and the three-legged dog of sadness
that paws at my heels with his purple claws.

What were we but an erring script
of moan (

when together
and alone

).
Have you bedded the librarian yet?

Laid him down in the Q's like a doe?
Felt the systemic crunch of his slow

paper hump? — when I said "get a life"
I meant with no one other than me.

The hardest edge fades not
its proper sheath

yet all metal man-handled
comes to cut this careless flesh.

Somewhere between the expected
and the real, as between the calendar

and the day, not one nor t'other, lies some reason.
Your astrolabe, attune it with the stars,

the way you would a tv.
If you are still looking for order,

you need go no further than the Greeks,
their servile chaos. I, for one,

along with Pope Gregory XII,
give you the gift of time.

It will not be exact
but it will be handsome,

a performance more pandering than most.
I send it to you

from under the unmoving
gnomon of solitude.

    v.

Of solitude I said these lives serve
no one but run all night through us

as the metro does,
enamoured with destination.

Did I say I was proper
or even political?

Or that I would support you as you rose
like a sunset against it all?

Or that I would not turn the dogs
in your direction? How hard

true sorrow hits. You humour the powerless
so they will dine with you when they rule.

Yet which loaf of bread? Which sauce?
Which order? Whom first do you serve?

Write your decrees carefully for
no one can trust their mood.

Here, let me bring the flowers from the fridge.
Am I wearing my hat right?

Does the piano wire show?
I know there *is* a logic

to the grocery-store stoicism of yours.
Yet why sharpen every knife

to be used against you? Save that speech
for the epilogue

for we've seen it,
we've already seen

so much,
expected you

so long.

VI.

So long for me, cry out my name
in the empty cathedral of your night.

I won't hear. I never did.
Whose job is this anyway

and why haven't we unionized?
Everybody wants to be a drummer

in the band. Even the unplanned has a master.
And those added points for thinness of exposure,

hard-handed one-upmanship?
We are not on the edge of it,

never were,
but following its smooth contours,

congruent with attention, curved calculus
of light over water. I am an important man,

I could say *an intellectual*.
I recycle, read books,

adultery is part of my master plan,
yet I pay for these things — every day —

for the beauty of the slow defeat,
giving myself up for time

and the retort's torturous whim.
Ash upon young coal,

shamed by what I share,
by what I know,

I am o
(in this line my one life spent).

So, for once, relinquish. Haul off. Push.
Give it all back to the mystery (misery),

the capital and liturgy (lethargy).
Let us feed the government of repose

with our degraded malease
and rally to my penultimate

disappointment.
There is no other way of being

so wrong and yet so right.
But support me with your calls,

your prayer wheels,
leave flowers at the hill

of my melodic sojourn.

VII.

Of my melodic sojourn,
make their oars into violins

so they can hear us play! Their forests?
Into newspapers, tacked to the trees!

In all of history, there has never been
so much waste, infinity and the forgotten

rules of the random
have out-planned us, manoeuvre

our every science. So much to fill
with this lusty, indeterminate hunger

for the unknown, something verging
on the eternal yet backing off, scared

of the possible knives and forks of domestication
for it's their dreams you've reamed,

you've rimmed, you've rhymed,
you bastard. Their lives are not a plaything!

But can we still distil to that fatal moment
when we mouth the apocalypse

and the epigraph to some shitty novel?
Another god writing promises

in invisible ink
(only a grand forecast of rain

is liable to get Him excited again)?
Am I the only one who knows

how it feels? I mean, is this a sentence
or an art?

A verdict, perhaps,
but not the rumblings of the galleon

heaving from port without us.
Surely not. Surely? Friend, stay.

Stay! Don't worry. Don't think
of that 17th-century life of adventure.

Let your money and your industry
put you to a restful sleep.

Retract your claws, pussycat.
What kind of heroes were we,

anyway?

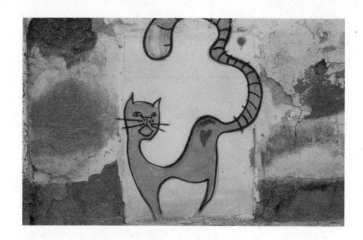

S hane Rhodes is the author of *The Wireless Room*, which won the Alberta Book Award for poetry, and *Holding Pattern*, which won the Archibald Lampman Award. He has published chapbooks, poetry, reviews, articles, and essays in magazines, anthologies, and newspapers across Canada. In addition to this, Rhodes has worked as an editor with *filling Station*, *The Fiddlehead*, and *Qwerty*. He lives in Ottawa, Canada, and writes wherever.